# Upstate Trilogy

# Upstate Trilogy

*A Celebration of Creation, Creativity, and the Examined Life from the Other New York*

T. P. BIRD

RESOURCE *Publications* • Eugene, Oregon

UPSTATE TRILOGY
A Celebration of Creation, Creativity, and the Examined Life from the Other New York

Copyright © 2024 T. P. Bird. All rights reserved. Except for brief quotations in critical publications or reviews, no part of this book may be reproduced in any manner without prior written permission from the publisher. Write: Permissions, Wipf and Stock Publishers, 199 W. 8th Ave., Suite 3, Eugene, OR 97401.

Resource Publications
An Imprint of Wipf and Stock Publishers
199 W. 8th Ave., Suite 3
Eugene, OR 97401

www.wipfandstock.com

PAPERBACK ISBN: 979-8-3852-2887-4
HARDCOVER ISBN: 979-8-3852-2888-1
EBOOK ISBN: 979-8-3852-2889-8

09/03/24

Scriptures are from THE HOLY BIBLE, NEW INTERNATIONAL VERSION®, NIV® Copyright © 1973, 1978, 1984, 2011 by Biblica, Inc.® Used by permission. All rights reserved worldwide.

To all my old neighbors and friends
in upstate New York,
a beautiful and inspiring place

# Contents

### PART ONE: WHILE CREATION WAITS FOR PERFECT FREEDOM

| | |
|---|---:|
| Introduction: While Creation Waits for Perfect Freedom | 3 |
| Winter on Post Creek | 4 |
| Moonstruck | 5 |
| Sugar Hill Triptych | 6 |
| Two Seasons on the Finger Lakes Trail | 8 |
| Dining Out | 9 |
| Lights | 10 |
| Subject to Frustration | 11 |
| A Splendid Late Evening Show | 13 |
| Celebration | 15 |
| Field Notes while Walking Buck Hollow Road in June* | 16 |
| While Atop an Unnamed Arcadian Hill* | 18 |
| On My Visit with Future Preachers of Nature's Gospel | 20 |
| A Busy July Evening | 22 |
| A Mid-Summer Tale about Cows | 23 |
| A Small Poem (Somewhat) about Lunch | 24 |
| A Poem about Three Frogs in a Pond | 26 |
| From the Railroad Track in Beaver Valley | 27 |

## Contents

| | |
|---|---|
| On the Trail to Dunning Pond* | 30 |
| Tapestry | 32 |
| Anatomy of an Old Fallen House | 33 |
| A Meeting with a Whitetail Deer | 35 |
| Transitioning | 36 |
| Storm Front | 38 |
| Observations and Musings at Siglin's Pond* | 39 |
| Cinnamon Lake Soundings* | 41 |
| That's Intertainment! | 42 |
| After the Rain Has Stopped | 44 |
| Another Autumn Poem | 45 |
| Anticipation | 47 |
| Visit to an Old Graveyard in the Sugar Hill State Forest | 49 |
| November Interlopers | 51 |
| Climbing Sugar Hill in Early Winter | 52 |
| A Walk in Winter Woods | 54 |
| *Epilogue:* Nature Pays a Visit | 56 |

### PART TWO: IDA'S VISION

| | |
|---|---|
| Introduction: Ida's Vision | 59 |
| "At Nash Lake, August 14, 1899" | 62 |
| "Wood Cutters, 1900" | 64 |
| The Elegant Lady | 66 |
| "Bath, Saturday, July 14, 1901" | 68 |
| Young Harold among the Chickens, 1901 | 70 |
| Ida and Harold, June 1904 | 72 |
| "Sheep Shearer, May 23, 1905" | 75 |
| "Aunt and Lamb, 1905" | 77 |
| "Waders in Post Creek, 1905" | 80 |
| "Track Gang, 1905" | 82 |
| Post Creek Temperance Meeting | 85 |
| Grocer F. H. Coger's Delivery Man | 88 |

## Contents

Winter Photos: Ida, Forrest, the Horses, and a Sledge ... 90
"Three Sisters, 1912" ... 93

### PART THREE: LOST SENTIMENTS

Introduction: Lost Sentiments ... 97
*Prologue:* A Man at Forty-Something ... 99
To Transcend or Not to Transcend, That's Not Really
  the Question ... 101
Upstate Heat Wave ... 102
The Character of Trees ... 103
Once Upon a Time, a Singer, Songwriter ... 104
A Strange Compulsion ... 105
Mindful ... 106
Emeline Davenport ... 107
Roads and Journeys ... 108
As One Looks at Marriage ... 110
Market Street Observations ... 111
The Blizzard ... 113
Weather Report ... 114
Civilization ... 115
Notes from a Summer Park* ... 117
Do the Ghosts of Old Farmers Still Watch the Weather?
  (A True Story)* ... 119
A Search for the Sublime among the Far Less Than Profound ... 120
Dill's Balm of Life ... 122
A Sunday Afternoon at Seneca Lake ... 124
A Casual Resume ... 126

# PART ONE

## While Creation Waits for Perfect Freedom

*Field Notes of an Upstate Day Hiker and Poet*

*A Celebration of the Creation*

"For the creation was subjected to frustration...
in hope that the creation itself will be liberated
from its bondage to decay and brought into
the glorious freedom of the children of God."

—From the Apostle Paul's Letter to the Romans

# Introduction
## While Creation Waits for Perfect Freedom

Living in upstate New York for thirty-five years, I spent as much free time as possible roaming private and public woods, hiking old farm and logging roads, marked state trails—following streams, my nose, and whatever else interested me. I was a day hiker, sometimes *all* day when I could. Sometimes my haunts were close to home—other times an auto trip away. Most were in the Finger Lakes region, others in western New York and the Adirondack Park. I was a fortunate fellow living in rural areas, enjoying the many state-land trails and old roads, recording what I saw, heard, and experienced of nature and its stories around me.

The following poems are composed from my field notes extending through several notebooks from 1989 to 2007. The notebook entries extended a few years after I left the Empire State in 2009. However, the poems in this collection were occasioned in upstate New York, except for two: one in northern Pennsylvania while on vacation, and the other in Kentucky (I couldn't resist). The poems are set month to month, but not year to year, from three different homes in upstate that I and my family lived in over the years. I hope the following will bring some pleasure to the reader; I must admit I probably took greater pleasure in pursuing my avocation and putting my adventures in verse and prose poems. As the old saying goes: "You had to be there"; hopefully the reader may feel like they were.

## WINTER ON POST CREEK

The early January snow falls silently—
making no sound in an almost silent world,
except for the crunch beneath my boots and
the slight tinkle against my parka's hood.

My dog and I walk the banks of Post Creek—
cold water running through and around
thin sheaths of velvety ice, small patches
of slush moving in the current like adventurous

men in rafts rowing through gurgling eddies
and small whirlpools. The air is still and cold—
a white lace curtain across the sky and filling
the earth until both begin to meet as one

in a veil of fading light and falling snow.
Once back home I place fresh straw in the
dog's coop, and she enters quickly to rest
and warm herself after a bracing winter's walk.

# MOONSTRUCK

January 20th, 11:00 p.m. . . .
I watch a total eclipse of the moon
high in the cold dark heavens—
the shadows of its craters like vague
facial features behind a thin orange veil.
In this moment I am literally stuck
in the middle between Sol and Luna.

Around 3:00 a.m. . . .
awakened by an unknown signaling,
unable to sleep, I rise in silence from our bed.
From a downstairs window I watch
from the darkness of the kitchen
two small doe in the bright moonlit snow,
chew low hanging branches of our apple tree.

If all this were being filmed for a movie,
I would have "Moonlight Serenade," or
something similar, playing lightly in the
                      background.

## SUGAR HILL TRIPTYCH

*Stirrings*

Late winter and the pond ice is still thick
but pocked by the warmer rays of a sun
come nigh.

The breeze sings a new song—though it struggles
against a crow's arrogant cackle, while water,
freed within the earth, rambles on

about the places it's been—a story it tells
over and over again until someone
listens with solicitude.

The naked woods snap and crackle with
the movement of small animals.
Black-capped chickadees

flit among the tiny bones of sleeping trees
like nervous commuters. It's a day of
secret stirring in a season of unrest.

And does this include the stirring of hearts
that once lived among these trees,
who sat beside this water,

waiting for the spring to arrive again?

## Foundations

Foundations found in the sleep of winter—
slumbering quietly in dreams of work,
sweat, play and laughter—

memories forgotten except a stranger walking
in his present time finds the objects
of their remembrance:

rusty tools to continue one's labor in the fields
of heaven and dirt filled jars to store
the meaning of a once earthly life.

## Ghosts

White birches at dusk—ghosts walking abroad
among empty cellars now shallow holes
open to an evening sky, filled with

pink puffy clouds trimmed in dusty charcoal.
And here are ghosts walking among
ghosts assigned to hold hands

with each other, forced to finally concede
the sum of things ruled or possessed
never equals the number of days

given and lived as a gift.

*Originally published in my chapbook,* Scenes and Speculation *(Finishing Line Press), now revised.*

# TWO SEASONS ON THE FINGER LAKES TRAIL

I.
Early March, 2:30 p.m. I'm taking a rest and eating lunch by a running stream, its waters like a subway train under a surface of ice and snow that glints beneath a weak winter sun before disappearing into turning shadows. A sunlit, mold-green boulder serves as my seat; it reminds me of a giant tortoise, or perhaps, more a patient Buddha waiting for travelers like myself to come and sit awhile. For this feels like a place of esoteric, possibly spiritual, thought: the gurgling stream—its waters, like the blood flowing through my arteries, through my brain—causing me to respond to nature's forces. Its waters, once circulating through the heart of the sleeping earth, are soon to awake as I am now awake to its coming renewal, and both impatient as the wind.

II.
Early May, 9:23 a.m. I'm back on the "Buddha rock," the snow and ice are gone, the sterile smell of winter replaced by the scent of spring. The trees are budded, but a bit behind the ones down in the valleys. The waters of the stream speak a clearer language—now freed from encrusted ice—despite the hidden sun behind flat, gray clouds that dominate the sky. What thoughts may this day bring as I contemplate the direction of life's changes? Then, a strange sound in the distance. I believe it to be a wild turkey. Yes, the definite sound of a hen's calling. Yet, I know, certainly not for me.

## DINING OUT

Late March...
We have a visitor
this evening at
our compost pile.

Mr. Possum is
having dinner out—
courtesy of our
family's scraps.

He sits contented in
the twilight, gnawing
away at some choice,
rotting morsel.

Apparently satiated,
off he promenades
across the sheared
cornfield, and toward
the nearby creek.

According to the rules
of nature, there is nothing
like fine dining at an
exclusive compost pile.

## LIGHTS

> *"Arise, shine, for your*
> *light has come,*
> *and the glory of the Lord*
> *rises upon you."*
>
> —Isaiah 60:1

At the last of April,
looking up at the top
of a yellow birch—
its new, pale leaves,
blown about
in a strong breeze—
appear as
little gold lights
twinkling in the
evening sunlight.

It would appear...
in this new season
all things are drawing
toward the light.
There is no reason
to live in the cold
regret of winters past.

## SUBJECT TO FRUSTRATION

1.

Early May . . .
while walking the creek
behind my mother-in-law's house.

I sit on a fallen tree to watch
a large flying ant struggle
to lug a brown spider—
backwards—across dead, dry grass.
It's determined to complete its mission.

2.

Late August . . .
while resting in a lean-to on the FLT.

A bee has got itself caught in a spider's
web. I watch it frantically beat its wings—
trying to extricate itself from the sticky
filament.

The resident spider sits quietly at the far
end; she is in no hurry—just waiting
for the bee to wear itself out.

Finally the desperate hymenopter is
down to one free wing, body still
convulsing in the tangled web.

Now, slowly the spider approaches—
moves from behind the struggling bee,
maneuvering to inject its deadly venom.

Soon, it will be all over.

## A SPLENDID LATE EVENING SHOW

Late May . . .
Sitting on a fallen tree on the abandoned side
of a once twin railroad bed, I watch
nature's splendid late evening show . . .

Like a late spring snowstorm—
drifting dandelion seeds fill the air, now
filtered through the red lens of low evening
sunlight—just now coming over a distant hilltop.

The air also jumps heavy with newly hatched
insects, bobbing and weaving in bunches—
especially over the wetlands alongside the track,

Red-wings fly back and forth through bushes and
small trees—chattering, gurgling—full of early
season excitement.

Swallows swoop to and fro, up and down
through the hordes of bugs right over my head
in their own instinctive choreography.

A couple of goldfinches streak through the throng,
looking for a snack. They're all eating good tonight.

A pair of mallard ducks fly an oval pattern
parallel to the tracks—appearing to be in a race.
I can't say who will win.

There is much sight and sound from
sun, seeds, birds and bugs in this early
preview of coming summer evenings.

And best of all—the show is free!

## CELEBRATION

*"You teach me the way of life.
In your presence is total celebration.
Beautiful things are always
in your right hand."*

—Psalm 16:11

A long, dangling wildflower
with little white blossoms is
growing in the crook of a
dead limb on an old maple.

In God's economy . . .
nature makes space for new
life to thrive—even in the
arms of yesterday's beauty.

*Gloria in excelsis Deo!*

## FIELD NOTES WHILE WALKING BUCK HOLLOW ROAD IN JUNE*

I write my wanderings in my notebook—which rests on a locus fencepost "desk," which I share with insects and a yellow spotted caterpillar—who, no doubt, puzzles at my presence in the very place he calls his own.

1.
Today, a high wind runs atop these green hills.
A constant rush of sound issues through trees, shrubs and grass—all acting as a reed in nature's woodwind instruments.

A distant roar and a nearer whoosh form a capacious symphony of music in my ear. Then the wind suddenly dies to an instant silence . . . and, quickly returns.
Even in nature's concert hall, there is a pause between musical parts. I then wonder . . .

how many insect, bird, and animal lives are being wrought out in the thick, grassy pasture waving at my feet. I think of untold lives behind drawn blinds in faraway cities—all played out in small, hidden places.

Out of sight are most of our stories, never written down, the majority left behind with the dead—just like the forgotten family Buck, who long ago gave its precious name to this dusty country road in upstate New York.

2.
I notice an oasis of lilac and wild rose—indicating a
way station on the journey of history. The bones of
this homestead lie quiet; it is the way of man's time
and circumstance. For here a frost-scattered footing
of fieldstone lies buried within the roots of these bushes—
in soil that has lost its memory of kinship with the family
who once planted in expectancy of an annual blessing.

3.
Further down the road where a small stream runs its
way along side, and the woods are thin and sun-dappled—
a toilet bowl sits like a giant porcelain mushroom in the
wet, mossy ground. Mans' technology meets nature's
running water, and becomes a picture of contemporary
rural America. This bowl is like a monument to progress.

4.
I have disturbed a small garter snake sunning itself
in the grass-line by the stream. He lies quiet as a stick,
waiting for me to compose my jolted thoughts.
What are *his* jolted thoughts as he warily surveys me—
his little pebble-like head arched slightly above his body,
his thread-like tongue testing the air between us?

Apparently, we have agreed to be both mutually disturbed,
*and* curious on this summer day—both man and reptile
concurring to move on to the rest of our respective lives.

*Originally published in my chapbook,* Scenes and Speculation *(Finishing Line Press), now revised.*

## WHILE ATOP AN UNNAMED ARCADIAN HILL*

Standing atop this treeless hill,
the early June sun clear and hot—
a breeze cools my skin against
the unaccustomed warmth after a
northern winter and a cool spring.

A tractor works hard somewhere
on a nearby, unseen knoll. It chugs
and snorts like a mechanical ox
against its yoke—its unsung driver
quite oblivious to my wanderings.

Yellow wildflowers dot the ground
at my feet and well beyond the swell
of my breath. Tiny insects dive and
swirl around me—King Kong on the
"state" building of their pastoral city.

At a moderate distance and across
a small dale, an appealing tree line
runs atop a long ridge. From here
they spread a pencil width apart.
On either side, the rise is open turf.

A strange urge captivates me—
a longing to rest beneath the
shadowy coolness of those trees.
Perhaps, deep thoughts and sublime
verse await me there to discover.

Surely, the ridge's grass is greener,
a mind likely to be clearer, more
discerning. Oh, wanderlust ranging
from hilltop to hilltop. Sitting there,
would I long to be where I am now?

*Originally published in my chapbook,* Scenes and Speculation *(Finishing Line Press), now revised.*

## ON MY VISIT WITH FUTURE
## PREACHERS OF NATURE'S GOSPEL

Late June . . .

stepping off the Finger Lakes Trail
I enter a small glade of tall trees—

narrow, very straight, bearing few limbs—
except at the top, where leaves form

a canopy like a stained-glass window
through which the sun dapples the ground

below. Here in this natural forest chapel
is a rotted trunk of a large fallen tree—

like a much used pew. In a hollowed out area
filled with wet, fertile forest debris—

grow a number of *jack-in-the pulpits*,
immature, not yet having blossomed.

They appear as young, attentive divinity
students eager to hear a lesson, perhaps a

story from their learned professors. However,
I have no ready story to tell these neophyte

woodland preachers. As I start to leave,
a bird begins chirping loudly, as if to say,

"wait a while longer!" It is then I remember
the psalmist's exhortation . . .

*Be still and wait upon the Lord.*

## A BUSY JULY EVENING

With Skipper, my black cocker spaniel, enjoying a beautiful sunny evening, the air cool, refreshing after a humid spell. We watch a lot of avian activity—flying, sitting, landing and taking off. It's like a busy airport: *waxwings, doves, sparrows, thrushes, red-wings, finches, swallows, raucous kingfishers, a flicker, two mallard ducks*—all either transversing field and pond or tapping at a tree; most looking for tasty insect morsels, or energy producing seeds. Soon, another image comes to mind: that of a busy bird-land marketplace with prices at an all time low!

But now . . . my attention gets diverted from bird to beaver . . . he swims in the pond—at a distance from his hut in the swampy suburbs—back and forth, back and forth with his nose held out of the water like the prow of a boat—not more than twenty to twenty-five feet from us. In my field glasses, he is within an arm's length. Yet, he shows no apparent alarm at our presence—occasionally slapping his tail on the water and diving—reappearing on the surface a few yards away. I turn to my left to see Skipper's reaction to Mr. Beaver—only to spot two great blue herons low in the sky just beyond her. I've never seen two of these giant birds together, or so close. What a marvel they are! What a marvel it *all* is!

## A MID-SUMMER TALE ABOUT COWS

A lady in a little red car
is taking photos of Holstein
cows atop Catlin Hill—they

being particularly photogenic
due to the higher altitude—
their noses a brighter pink, their

eyes a more mellow brown, their
black and white a perfect mix.
But, understand: this doesn't

make them more contented cows—
just prettier before a camera lens
on a lovely summer day.

I believe this is what the lady in
the little red car really cares about.
As for the cows, heaven only knows.

## A SMALL POEM (SOMEWHAT) ABOUT LUNCH

1.

Mid-July...
Observing through binoculars
a male bob-o-link in a grassy
field adjacent to Saylor Road.

He holds a small orange moth
in his beak while jumping from
stalk to stalk and shuffling down
to get a better grip.

Like this bird, some people are just
choosy about at which table they eat
                their lunch.

2.

In the woods off Saylor Road
I've found a caterpillar, about two
inches long, brown, with a set of feet
in front and four in back.

It clings to the side of a tree—arched
over backwards like an acrobat or gymnast—
hanging from its rear feet.

It appears to be taking a nap.

I poke, but it refuses to admit my presence—
probably hoping I think it a twig, or a
                piece of bark.

However, what it might not know—
I have no intention of having him or her
for my lunch, even if I had found
the perfect table to do so.

## A POEM ABOUT THREE FROGS IN A POND

Mid July . . .
Three large green and yellow frogs sit together
in a hidden mucky pond—bulging eyes and
blank expressions on their froggy faces—skin

glowing magnificently in the low evening sun.

Are they siblings, friends, or just strangers waiting
for a conversation to begin before the daylight ends?
What would frogs have to say after such a boggy day?

Is one a handsome prince cursed into amphibian life,
waiting on a fair maiden to kiss his froggy lips—the
others destined to always be a frog in a mucky bog?

What do frogs think about while laying in the algaed
water right up to their froggy lips and more?
Perhaps: "Gee, it's certainly a glorious boggy day—

I'd hate to be a prince stuck in a castle all the while!"

# FROM THE RAILROAD TRACK IN BEAVER VALLEY

1.
Late July. A pastoral scene: early evening,
the sun is lowering in the western sky.

In the rosy sunlight and bug filled air
a small group of mourning doves rise
from their supper roost in a newly cut
field and fly cheerily over rows of
baled hay.

It seems nature's version of dinner and a movie.

2.
A blue heron rises from a small pond,
flying away at my approach.

Deciding not to be intimidated, the great bird
with a saber-like beak and fashion model's legs
returns as I observe from my seat on the end
of a railroad tie.

*Live and let live* must be his thought
on such a splendid summer's eve.

3.
I hear a classic avian voice, and spot a
belted kingfisher through my field glasses.

He sits atop a tall dead tree and sends
a white jet-stream from beneath his
tail feathers, while taking off over the track-
side swamp—all as if to say...

"Take that, you nosy human voyeur!"

4.
I looked upon the beaver hut
in the swampy area just north of the pond.
No sign of Mr. Beaver...
he is either inside sleeping, or off looking
for choice branches on which to sharpen his
teeth and fill his stomach.

I see no reason to leave a calling card;
he has seen me watching him swim these waters
a number of times before.

5.
I see through my field glasses a doe
with two fawns cross the tracks—most likely
to get a drink from Post Creek.

About to enter the brush along the stream,
she stops—either spotting my presence or
                      catching my scent.
She hesitates, then waits in stillness—trying to
get a fix on what alarmed her.

Making up her mind, she turns back across
the tracks and off like a shot she runs, her two
youngsters bouncing along behind, little white
                                  flags flying.

The drink can wait until the stranger has gone.

# ON THE TRAIL TO DUNNING POND*

A gentle stream moves slowly
along the trail—its liquid voice
gurgles and plunks its way
across moss covered rocks.

Water striders glide atop the
calm surface of deeper pools
like Sunday afternoon pleasure
craft on a favorite hidden lake.

Nearby narcissistic ferns bow
down to view their reflections
in the water where a big green
and brown frog pretends not to

notice their hubris. Woodland
birds, upon a stranger's arrival,
dart from tree top to tree top.
Except for an occasional chirp

or twitter, they are silent and
secretly watchful. At the pond
small fish dart just below the
surface as a noisy kingfisher

heralds the stranger's advance.

A salamander sits on a rock shelf
just below the water line, while
turquoise damselflies hover above,

patrolling their territory.
Just then—not to be outdone, two
USAF jets streak low overhead
as if protecting this pond from

human intrusion. Nature is never far
from the shadow of man's machines.

*Originally published in my chapbook, Scenes and Speculation (Finishing Line Press), now revised.*

# TAPESTRY

> *"See how the lilies of
> the field grow. They do not
> labor or spin. Yet I tell you
> that not even Solomon in all
> his splendor was dressed
> like one of these."*
>
> —Matt 6:28–29

An ordinary pasture on Whiteman's farm in early August has become a colorful country tapestry.

Against a glowing green background, wildflowers spread out in whites, yellows, purples, blues, browns, and pink—

to form an impressionist painting of *Queen Anne's lace, astor, brown-eyed susans, trefoil, clover, chicory, wild daisy, and milkweed.*

All are accented with the flitting movement of orange and black monarchs and the streaked brown and white of savannah sparrows.

The cares and worries of life fade away for me in this riotous display of nature's handiwork; all is under the watch of
the Artist's careful eye.

## ANATOMY OF AN OLD FALLEN HOUSE

Early August . . . I'm surprised to find
a fallen house on Locust Lane—
an old dirt road in the New York State Forest—
vacated sometime during the Great
                Depression of the 1930s.

Caved in on itself, it sits atop a crumbling
stone foundation—a two story affair that
might've been painted light yellow or white—
but now, a gray, dead hulk of many broken
bones—lathed ribs exposed, skin and muscle

long gone through physical collapse and
many seasons of sun, rain, snow, and freeze.
This wreck, once a family's home—
is slowly returning to its fundamental elements
as it retreats back into nature's open arms.

Standing on stone slabs—nearly buried in
layers of dead leaves and covered in moss—
I peer into the back entrance; no door,
its frame leaning at thirty degrees with wild
grape vines hanging over it like a torn curtain.

Inside the shell I see a hand-hewed beam
lie like an animal's spine—separated from
its wasted carcass. I'm oddly struck with
a feeling of sentiment upon noticing a few
unbroken window frames still showing

the faded blue of their last coating with paint.
I imagine a mister or missus carefully
spreading the color, then standing back
and thinking, *Yes, that's going to look just fine.*
And to my roving eyes it still holds its beauty.

## A MEETING WITH A WHITETAIL DEER

Eighth of August . . . while on vacation, out hiking on Barkley Mountain, an old nineteenth-century anthracite coal mining region in northern Pennsylvania. Remembering it's the anniversary of my mother's recent death, I feel downcast, even a bit lonely. As I stand on the top of a rise in an old slag field, I see a large whitetail come out of deep woods at less than a hundred yards. It stares at me; I stare back. It becomes anxious, moves about, snorts, and takes a few hesitant steps toward me. Without thinking, I whistle a tune. The whitetail stops, seems to calm down, continues to stare, appears to listen, then turns with another snort, reentering the deeper woods. It's curious that suddenly I feel some comfort.

# TRANSITIONING

Last week of August . . .
I'm here on a recently sheared
Catlin Hill meadow—sitting on

a square bale of prickly hay—
strangely placed among many
large and tightly coiled rolls.

The feel of high summer is fading;
occasional splashes of red in the
maples send a familiar signal.

The sun in the west appears a blotch
of reddish yellow in an odd, out of
focus way—as if it's trying to make

up its mind on how to appear.
Under an ostensibly bluer sky,
streaked with high cirrus clouds,

a hawk soars over the trees lining
the newly cut field. He seems to fly
less hindered in the evening air that

moves upon me with less moisture
in its touch—it being almost cool
against my unaccustomed summer skin.

Perhaps my strong feelings for
autumn's glory exceed the pace of
seasonal cycles? Yet, I'm sure,

I sense the tired summer fading—
If just enough to tantalize.

## STORM FRONT

Late August . . . my wife and I start from the car—walking east on Pearl Street, a country road near the small farming village of Moreland. The sun is out, yet, the strong wind makes it a day unsure if it's warm or cool. Soon, from the west, a wall of black clouds appears in the sky—having an edge as sharp and defined as a knife. As we sit under a tree in front of an old rundown farmhouse, we watch it move over us like a massive line of dark warriors or, perhaps, a huge wave in a stormy sea. High upper winds move it swiftly past. Seen from behind, the leading edge gives off a trailing orange glow.

Thoughts turn to science-fiction movies, where aliens travel in dark storm clouds with bolts of lightening, ready to wreak havoc on us poor unsuspecting earthlings. Yet, this storm front is not going to drop any rain on us—at least not yet, for we drive home under a clear evening sky. Apparently, there's no sure way to discover aliens, or even the result of a passing front. Sometimes, nature is like a magician—now you see it, now you don't. Perhaps designed by God to keep us on our toes.

## OBSERVATIONS AND MUSINGS AT SIGLIN'S POND*

Last day of August...
sitting at the edge of the woods
on the "thinker's bench,"
looking down on Siglin's Pond—
a small body hidden by trees and bushes
heavy with red berries.
The pond's water is full and healthy
under a sky layered in a low ceiling of
puffy clouds.

Lilies in full bloom float close to shore—
leaves on the surface bobbing gently
in the small currents made by the wind;
appearing as party guests, they move
in and out of conversations, circulating
slightly, as if looking for possibilities.

At my foot is a devil's paintbrush,
beside it, another small daisy-like flower.
Wryly, I wonder, what kind of gossip
would they share with each other—
seeing as they live in the same neighborhood?
That is of course, *if* wildflowers could talk.
And, if so, they would be like housewives
chin-wagging over a fence—that is, if flowers
had chins, *and* if there was a fence.

Would their conversation be different
from the water lilies some yards away?
Their respective lives, after all, would be
understood from different perspectives.

I realize it's time I stir from my
"thinker's bench," and move on to less
esoteric thoughts somewhere deeper
                        in the nearby woods.

*Originally published in* Tiny Seed Journal, *now revised.*

## CINNAMON LAKE SOUNDINGS*

Late summer wind journeys through tree tops
like the many voices of a chorus.

Crickets play their fiddles while songbirds
call out the dance.

Dragonflies swing back and forth—
the beat of their wings too fine to hear,

while others drum their tails like percussionists
against the surface of the water—

laying eggs with purpose and quite without shame
as other insects and bugs buzz and whine

like spirited socializers at a raucous party.
Even if I had to pay for this concert,

surely, it would not have mattered.
For the day is unto itself a song sweetly

sung for the benefit of all nature's glory.

*Originally published in my chapbook, Scenes and Speculation (Finishing Line Press), now revised.

## THAT'S INTERTAINMENT!

> *'Twas in the mild September,*
> *September, September,*
> *'Twas in the mild September,*
> *And the mocking bird was singing far and wide.*
>
> —FROM THE 1855 SONG "LISTEN TO THE MOCKINGBIRD"
> BY SEPTIMUS WINNER

While visiting my brother
at his new house in the suburbs,
we are entertained by a
neighborhood mockingbird.

He sits atop a neighbor's old TV
antenna—jumping up, fluttering
back down, changing his tune faster
than a disc jockey on an old top forty
radio show—or, my brother turning
the dial on the car radio every five
seconds as we travel down the highway.

As the old song tells us:
*Listen to the mockingbird,*
*Listen to the mockingbird.*

Whose tune might he have to sing?

And, on the subjective side . . .
what tune would *I* have him sing?

## AFTER THE RAIN HAS STOPPED

Early September,
somewhere in the
Beaver Dams State Forest . . .

Small frogs are plentiful
in the shallow pools collected
after recent rains. In fact,
this old logging road
appears to literally move
as these tiny creatures leap
for cover at my approaching
steps.

Could this be the road to
Pharaoh's ancient Egypt?

## ANOTHER AUTUMN POEM

Mid-October, I take account of this hilltop meadow,
freshly shorn and tightly wound into images of woolly
beasts upon the plain—framed in fading green into

reds and yellows, and lit from above with clear light
in a profound blue. Marbled clouds of an airy gray,
laze indifferently to the far north.

Upon the ground . . . the last bumble-bee is on the last
clover of the season. A small blossom grows yellow
and delicate in fresh deep green grass—wet with tiny

drops of water hiding in its shadows. Holstein cows—
like salt and pepper shakers set on cafe tables—
graze across the road, content in the crystalline

autumn light. Upon the back of a "woolly beast,"
someone has placed the skull of a tiny animal—long
gone to the natural history of this hill—its interior filled

with dirt and dead grass. I toss it back to earth where
it belongs. A feather, brown and thin, sets entangled in
the wound hay—its owner, possibly, gone to other skies

or somewhere fallen to earth. Yet, even when the mind is sharply focused on these eventualities, and life often uncertain and clumsily lived—a day like this makes one

glad for every breath taken from autumn's energizing air.

## ANTICIPATION

1.
Middle October. Red-wing
blackbirds in great numbers
are flying in swaying flocks
from harvested cornfield to
tree top and back again—all
in a great chatter of excitement—
bursting with raw energy,
and a strange avian nervousness.
Red patches flash like markings
on squadrons of fighter planes—
anticipating the leaving of their
local swampy abodes and their
forthcoming mission south.

2.
Late October afternoon in a
rust colored woods, leaves
falling one or two at a time
from summer trees—appearing
like poor children dressed
in ragged clothes.
Nature is quiet, as if holding its
very breath. The only sounds—
except for the occasional soft twill
of birds, are man's machines,

and their guns, rattling in the
distance. Nature is waiting in
the calm before the coming of
winter storms.

I too am waiting in anticipation,
and my waiting is also clear:
I'm waiting for the final end to
*all* of life's storms.

## VISIT TO AN OLD GRAVEYARD IN THE SUGAR HILL STATE FORREST

Taking a wrong turn on a trail through this New York State Forrest, I've come upon a neglected nineteenth-century graveyard of perhaps thirty sites situated atop a couple of steep knolls—discovered only with a quick glance to my left—through the late October trees.

I wonder... how many hikers have passed by—not knowing this small piece of the past lies hidden in these woods near Templar Road—a burial site now in the embrace of since-grown trees and woody plants? I took a wrong turn, and because I enjoy local history and old cemeteries,

I'm rewarded with a small glimpse into these forgotten people's lives...

I take note of the peculiar names of folks from an almost foreign time: Cornelius, Solomon, Rolina, Ebenezer, Silas, Dorcas, and many others. The oldest stone belongs to Thomas Nichols Sr., who died in 1847 at the age of sixty-one. The newest: 1919—that of Christiana Hicks,

whose husband, Solomon C. Hicks, passed away in 1864; after a long distance widowhood—they're together again, enclosed within a rusty cast iron fence. The plot for the Kendell family includes a memorial for a son—Oscar, a member of the 14th New York Regiment—

dying in Alexandria, VA, Oct. 24, 1864, at eighteen years.

His father, John, lived a long life—passing at eighty-four in 1905 after losing his wife, Amy, in 1868, and three other children—Frank, the last one, dying in 1899. As well as long, it must have been a hard life. Daniel C. Norris of Co. A, 141$^{st}$ Regiment, New York

Volunteers—age twenty-three, died at Minors Hill, VA, Jan. 6, 1863. It's unlikely he is buried under this marker. No other Norris name is inscribed in stone. Except for Thomas Nichols Sr., these people—living and dying in the second half of their American century—

were once the lifeblood of this land. Now, their bodies have returned to their raw elements, their dust like that of Creation's initial fire, their names a passing curiosity to those who happen to notice their graves aside a forrest path. Despite all of nature's beauty and life's

possible wonders, it's the way of all men and their earthly designs.

## NOVEMBER INTERLOPERS

Driving home on Route 69 near Towlesville.
A male pheasant struts slowly across the road

right in front of us—"cocky" as can be.
Defiant-like—he won't get out of our way!

Mr. skunk digs away in the field behind
the house—driving Annie, our dog, crazy!

Just dropping off to sleep—I'm awakened
to the eerie sound of coyotes howling.

Eleanor, our cat, leaves dead chipmunks
at our back door—two mornings in a row.

A garter snake hiding under the shed's Bilco
doors manages to startle me royally. Uh-huh.

All in all, living in the country has its moments,
and the kinds they be tend to become hazy in

                        the reckoning.

## CLIMBING SUGAR HILL IN EARLY WINTER

December, near the solstice.
The temperature is just above freezing.
I'm following an old sap-line up Sickler Road—
a steady climb over a shallow coating of wet snow
and melting ice on a rutted dirt surface. In places,

water runs in side ditches and across the lane, while
thawing snow drops from limbs above.
The winter sky is silver-gray—the air shrouded
in a light fog that gets thicker as I climb.

A gentle, yet damp wind forces me to lift the hood
on my parka. All is quiet, peaceful, almost ghostly—
except for busy chickadees darting across the road
into naked thickets.

Lots of turkey tracks underneath an old apple tree,
whose limbs still bear the shriveled, rotten remains
of last autumn's meager fare. Mottled and sunken red
fruit, a few withered berries, and dried leaves dangling

in a nearby black cherry, are nature's humble ornaments
hung for the Christmas season. When I reach the old iron
fire tower at the top of the hill, a fine blanket of mist
moves about in the chilled breeze like a restless spirit.

I sense much of nature is asleep and so, I pull my hood closer around my head, and keep watch in case its dreams unfold before me. I would not want to miss what awesome truths God might reveal as I rest body and soul before Him.

## A WALK IN WINTER WOODS

The sixth day of Christmas, I enter a trail
off Vanzandt Hollow Rd.—just above an
old bridge abutment and a small waterfall
on Glen Creek. My goal: to reach a pleasant,
hidden lake revealed to me last summer.

The air is cold, a light dusting of plumy snow
lays on the trail. A crisp breeze shakes
some wispy flakes loose from the limbs of
surrounding trees, sending about miniature
flurries within the naked, gray woods.

Glen Creek runs far below the trail in its
canyon course. Partially coated with ice—
a mottled, marble-like, frozen skin hides
frigid water flowing swiftly just beneath
its surface.

I hike the trail until it crosses another
rushing stream. The bridge is gone—washed
away in the swift running water. I slip on
snow-covered ice while searching to ford.
Down I go on my right elbow. With no place
to cross, hurting, angry and disappointed—

I turn around and hike back up the steep side
of a hollow I just came down. At the top I
lie down in a sudden burst of cold sunlight
and try to catch my breath, *and* rest my weary,
unwarranted temper.

Finding a set of boot tracks in the snow
veering off the trail and up an old logging road,
I, on the spur of the moment, decide to follow—
only to see them turn off to the right at a thick
pine grove, and into the woods.

Still in an ill-affected mood—I plunge stubbornly
ahead through the evergreens—thankfully,
hitting the trail again by the rim of the canyon.
A walk in winter woods can bring about
*the best of times, and, the worst of times.*

A day-hiker must live to learn from both.

## EPILOGUE: NATURE PAYS A VISIT

A Saturday morning, I'm sitting on the back porch, drinking a cup of tea while stroking the fur of the family cat, and staring at Skipper's empty doghouse—just days after putting her down. She was well-nigh to death from old age and a tumor in her belly. Hearing a loud knocking sound upon metal, I look about for its source. Finally, I spot a yellow-bellied sapsucker atop the metal cowling of our chimney. Every so often he began tapping his metal perch with his beak. I thought: was this in response to my wife typing inside the house near an open window—her keyboard tapping away like another possible sapsucker in the neighborhood?

Soon he was gone . . . yet, shortly, he came back—tapping away again like a fool. Then a sound came from our neighbor's chimney: a second sapsucker—doing the same thing on their cowling. Suddenly the yellow-bellied guy on our chimney swooped over and retrieved his companion from the neighbor's roof. Off they flew together—content at finding each other, and not the silly bird pecking at some computer keys.

# PART TWO

## Ida's Vision

*Narrative Poems Inspired by the Photos
of an Early Twentieth-Century Amateur Photographer*

*A Celebration of Creativity*

"It's not what you look at that matters,
it's what you see."

—Henry David Thoreau

# Introduction
## Ida's Vision

Sometime in the early 1980s, a friend, John Kent, introduced my wife and me to an old bachelor farmer—one Harold G. Stewart, who lived alone in his now aged and shabby farmhouse. It was his home since 1900—the year of his birth. His farm lay in northeast Steuben County in upstate New York, along side what is now NY 414 and Post Creek, which eventually empties south into the Chemung River at Corning. As a youth, and young man, John worked for Harold on the farm. Now, he and his wife periodically looked in on Harold and his needs, for Harold's housekeeper of many years had recently died.

Not long after, Harold asked John and his wife to move in with him. They had been living in a small log cabin on his mother's property since their marriage only a year or two before. Their reward would be the inheritance of the farm after Harold's death. In 1981 they nestled themselves in the old farmhouse with the old retired farmer. Because the Kent's invited us often for dinner or an evening of conversation and coffee, I got to know Harold, his birthplace, and home all the better.

Nothing had been done to modernize the old Stewart place—probably since the introduction of indoor plumbing and electricity some years before. Every room was filled with the detritus of his parent's life—besides the stuff Harold collected over his own eighty-five years. The upstairs rooms probably had not been used in many years—now filled with so much clutter making it hard to

## PART TWO: IDA'S VISION

get around. In many ways the house and property were a strange and unkept museum—somewhat stopped in time.

The L-connected cow and horse barns (Harold only used a tractor once over his long years of farming—it just did not suit him) still stood straight and strong, while many outbuildings were either gone or pitching to some point on the compass. Sheds remained connected to the back of the house—filled with junk, old tools, much what-have-you and yards of dirt and dust. Old implements lay buried in the tall grass of the barnyard.

John would not do any dairy farming, but would raise a few pigs, chickens, and four children—along with strange inventions of God only knows what, made from scraps of metal left around on the farm. To my knowledge they never worked. John was a most unusual fellow.

Spurred on by my many questions, Harold told me much about his life spent living on and working his land. Small stories and anecdotes would surface and develop out of his long-term memory. Many concerned his mother and father, Ida and Forrest, and himself growing up, working on the farm from his days as a young boy. Quite simply put, the farm was his life. His father died in 1920 at fifty-five, while his mother lived until 1951 to the age of eighty-two. It is she who inspired this collection of poems—all drawn from the photographs she left behind—taken from about 1899 to 1912.

I discovered her photos in a box hidden in the incredible wreckage of the second floor (part of the ceiling had fallen down). Many were faded with age or poor exposure, but a number were in excellent condition after eighty years. All were pasted on decorative white cardboard, some with notations on the back. What was her camera? Possibly a Kodak folding pocket camera or an early issue Kodak Brownie box camera; the former seems most likely. There were few "everyday use" cameras for the amateur available at the time.

Harold remembered little of his mother's avocation, and seemed disinterested in my admiration of her aesthetic skills. In

## INTRODUCTION

time he simply said, "Take what you want." And I did. Harold died in 1985.

In these vignettes I wish to honor Ida Stewart, an early twentieth-century farmer's wife who recorded her world through photography with uncommon artistic passion and surprising skill; she revealed the everyday life of a farm family who worked the soil and sold milk to the local dairy cooperative. She also photographed extended family, friends, and neighbors who shared life with her.

I know little or nothing of the context of these photos, but their images evoke in my imagination stories—stories that I wished to develop and share through *Ida's Vision*. Each piece begins with a description of Ida's photograph. What follows is my imagining of the picture's story in both prose-poem and narrative verse. I only hope they come up to the standards that Ida showed in her photographs.

## "AT NASH LAKE, AUGUST 14, 1899"

Ida does not identify the young woman who wades in the shallow water just offshore, where three clusters of vegetation reveal a hearty summer's growth. She leans over in a long-sleeved shirtwaist—to touch with her right hand, the nearest plant to Ida's camera—possibly, to pluck a flower. Was it by chance Ida fixed her subject on film between the farther two clusters? Seemingly, a perfect composition—one would think not by chance but of concentration. The right side of the woman's long dark skirt dips in the water, while she hikes the left—exposing a bold look of a black stockinged shin. Clutched in her hem-lifting hand is a straw hat pressed against her cloaked thigh. Perhaps this photograph came after another: two young girls on the seat of a wagon, with what looks like a large melon. Ida, with camera, faces two large horses, head on—all harnessed up, ready for a ride.

No men are around, inhibiting her daring late nineteenth-century venture into the water to explore the plants,
with their lovely flowers.

It's an outing of Ida's friends, a brave excursion
without male escorts farther into the town of Hornby—
northwest over the hill from the Stewart farm.

It's a Sunday picnic, a day away from household
chores and domestic concerns.
With laughter, singing, and gossip among the picnickers,

it's a heady trip over dirt roads past farms,
small hamlets and denuded hills.
Neighbors wave at the ruckus going by,

or shake their heads at such blatant Sabbath breaking.
A young woman in Ida's photograph will soon be
wading the shoreline of Nash Lake—

perpetually picking a flower from a watery plant.
Her day will not be affected at all by
who will see her daring black stocking.

## "WOOD CUTTERS, 1900"

Ida called this picture in a penciled note—"Wood Cutters." A woman holds a crosscut saw over a tree limb lodged in the arms of a crude sawhorse—a forthcoming sacrifice to the capricious god of fire. Body bent at forty-five degrees, her voluminous house-dress and apron hang loose—awry at the angle and effort of her work. Appearing too far from her work, losing the best possible leverage with the saw—is this a staged scene, a tableau set by the photographer? The natural slow-fixed exposure of Ida's camera should leave a blur of motion—if the saw was actually moving. Perhaps she is just starting to saw, or merely resting between strokes, and Ida then clicks the shutter? All conjecture. To the left and farther back, two younger females are in the picture. They sit on a log, while the one cuts alone. The person on the far left, who pins up her hair—possibly a young girl. Shirkers? Resting? All this is against a background of a rickety barn and stockade fence set in the shade of numerous trees. The scene does not appear to be at the Stewart farm.

The older two women are Martha and Mary—
like in Luke's gospel story.
Martha works alone the two-man saw.

She needs but a few chunks to light the summer stove.
Martha—annoyed that her sister is just sitting by,
says to their visitor,

"Ida, tell my sister to help me cut this wood."
But Ida only adds to Martha's frustration,
for Ida is of Mary's mind, and now—in a mood to tease.

"Oh, it is such a nice afternoon Martha.
I think Mary has chosen the better thing—
sitting and enjoying the summer day,

instead of sweating under its fractious sun."
Martha, with verve, quickly says,
"What kind of supper will a cold stove make?"

Here, Mary laughs and joins in the fun.
"A cold supper, Martha, a cold supper.
Besides, I'm keeping company with our guest."

Martha, not amused, says,
"Will father want a cold supper, Mary?"
Mary says nothing. Ida takes the picture,

and leaves the sisters to work out their sibling rivalry.

# THE ELEGANT LADY

## *(Possibly 1900)*

Who is the lady elegantly dressed in dark taffeta, a fur piece covering her shoulders, rising up the back of her neck? Ida has not penciled in a name or date on the photo's back. The lady wears a fashionable feathered hat of the times, which juts out over her forehead like a hood ornament on a mid-twentieth-century automobile. Although her hair is dark, the lady does not appear to be young—perhaps late middle-aged. Ida's subject stands in profile, facing to the right of the photograph, holding an infant. The child, wrapped in light colored blankets, faces in the same direction. A buggy's left front wheel and part of its raised canopy are shown behind her at a slight angle. The white head of a horse appears from behind the lady's back, its tail sprouting out from behind the baby's blankets. The head and shoulders of a man in a soft cap rise up in the distance near the front porch of the Stewarts' house. Is it early spring or the fall of the year? This is the only known photo where Ida gets her shadow in the picture.

Ida has baby Harold bundled up
against the autumn weather;
the sun is out, but she fears the ride to the church

in the family buggy may be too chilly
for the recently born infant.
Ida is having Harold baptized.

Though not particularly religious,
she feels it's not a bad idea to have
her child start out in life with good intentions.

Ida's mother *is*, and so *appears*, uncomfortable
holding Harold—facing him away,
secretly afraid he will spit-up on her elegant dress.

She knows this is not how a grandmother should act.
But, she is who she is, and has not the will
or strength to change.

At that moment Ida, sensing her mother's state of mind,
quickly takes a picture, and so rescues her
from her curious burden.

But she does not consider the position of the sun:
her shadow, like a dark spirit, falls against the taffeta dress
and the buggy's wheel like an omen of Harold's

seemingly long, lonely life—not to mention,
for the existence of this family photo.

## "BATH, SATURDAY, JULY 14, 1901"

One year old, Harold Stewart's bare body literally shines in the summer sun. He stands in a ragged lawn—a carpet that buries his feet in leaves of grass. His mother, Ida, has discretely taken his photograph from the rear, the little boy's buttocks, chubby like his legs—he is learning to walk convincingly upon the earth. A small wash tub and cloths are near. Are they wet or dry? In what condition do we find him in? A small orchard looms beyond the baby boy, a ladder climbing to the tree's highest fruit . . .

It's fruit, perhaps, like the fruit of
Adam's paradise lost.
It appears, as Adam and wife once walked naked,

young Harold, with curly towhead
and subtle placement of hands,
seems to luxuriate in *his* infant nakedness.

Does he unconsciously remember the freedom
of his mother's womb?
Are clothes not natural to his innocence—

like the first couple before their biblical fall
and expulsion from *Eden's* womb?
Here, young Harold looks to walk the earth—

even if unsteady, gazing upon things yet unknown.
He seems, at this moment, at least—
ready to leave behind fig leaves and garments of skin

to walk his chosen way.
This day was good, very good—
but before long, he will learn to walk

in fear and doubt—like the rest of creation's own.
And being fully clothed,
will be some kind of security over his life.

## YOUNG HAROLD AMONG THE CHICKENS, 1901

Is it before or after his outdoor summer bath? The former seems true, for young Harold stands in the midst of ever greedy chickens—no doubt enticed by the little boy with a handful of feed. He wears a white dress—common for a little boy of his age at this time in history, and looks toward Ida's camera with an impish smile. He appears as if to say, *look how cute and charming I am; but I really don't know why.*

Ida, needing to feed the chickens,
gives young Harold a handful of grain.
And so, he stands in his innocent dress,

a stranger among these feisty birds.
Yet, they will not allow such a thing to stand
in the way of their insatiable appetites.

For today, Ida has let Harold roam
a part of their farm's domain,
allowing him to become familiar

with the further environs of his new earthly home.
Little or no grass grows where chickens
peck the hen yard bare.

And, in his unshod feet the ground is extra foul
and dirty in the aftermath of their constant hunt,
and, quite so, their eventual elimination.

Does Ida think of her baby boy
perhaps stepping on a rusty nail,
a sharp stone, or tromping through the manure

of many hens?
Possibly. But, theirs is a rural life.
The farm is where they live intimately

with creatures of another kind,
their waste, their carnal ways,
along with the unknown bacteria of the earth.

Does Ida think much of health and hygiene
in an age of nescience?
If danger be a constant threat to stir the mind

to terrible distraction,
Ida could not live in this world that is her home.
And so, young Harold spends part of this summer day

among the greedy chickens.

## IDA AND HAROLD, JUNE 1904

Ida has created a self-portrait—including four-year-old Harold, and a large white cat at his feet. By whom the photo was snapped is not known. Her husband, perhaps? Yet, the composition is totally Ida. The farm's gambrel roof barns are in the far background, copulas and all—placed just off Ida's left shoulder and laterally above Harold's head. No longer is he a towhead, but now has dark hair like his mother. They stand at the corner of a fenced pasture that runs between Post Creek and the barns—Ida, body smartly posed at three-quarters to the camera, with her left arm laid across the top of the fencing. If we follow its direction, we see Harold, body facing full the camera, but looking down at the cat behind his right leg—allowing only part of his face to show. Ida wears a small collared, mid-shade printed dress (in a black and white photo), with many pleats from the bodice down. Her hair is pinned to the top of her head; a short tail trails. Harold is in mid-shade knee pants. Ida appears a young woman erect and confident in herself; Harold, still very much attached to his mother.

Ida, beforehand, peered through the eye
of her precious camera, and now knows
how she wants her picture to look.

"Can you see the barns clearly
in the background, Forrest?"
she asks.

Her husband says, "Yeah, I can see 'em alright."
Ida sighs, "No, I mean is anything blocking their view?"
Forrest just shakes his hat covered head.

A curious white cat enters the scene
without permission and occupies the boy's attention.
Ida turns to Harold.

"Stop fussing Harold, and be still."
And with another inhalation, says to Forrest,
"Make sure the fence post doesn't hide the barn door."

Forrest says nothing, but again shakes his head
at his wife's peculiar fastidiousness.
He is a farmer, not an "artist" like Ida,

and anxious to get back to his plow;
he already feels behind in his work.
The white horse, all hitched up and left behind,

does not mind the mid-day wait.
He's enjoying his rest, and the sweet grass
at the edge of the partially worked field.

"Well, if it looks good, go ahead and press the shutter.
Be careful now, don't shake the camera."
Forrest, way past impatient, presses the shutter.

Ida looks at her son, and sees he is
still messing with the curious white cat.
"Harold, did you look at the camera

while your father took the picture?"
With no word, Harold shrugs his small shoulders
hidden beneath his pullover shirt.

Forrest has already laid down the camera
in the grass and headed back to work.
Later Ida follows and snaps his picture—

standing behind his horse and plow
in a rock strewn field—
soon to be ready for the planting of corn.

## "SHEEP SHEARER, MAY 23, 1905"

Ida seems to have been acutely aware of, and interested in, all the things that went on around the farm and elsewhere. This included the man she labeled on the back of her May 1905 photo as "sheep shearer." He might have been her husband. Yet, to label the photo as she did, seems to suggest he was someone hired by her husband to do a "professional" job of yearly shearing the farm's flock of sheep. The "sheep shearer" stands erect in the doorway of a farm building—perhaps a barn; we cannot be sure. Darkness lies behind the man and the naked sheep he holds. It is a sunny day, for strong light falls on both man and sheep; shadows drop behind both man and beast until swallowed by the dark inside the building. Their length might suggest it be mid to late afternoon. A temporary table of sawhorses, and perhaps a door, sits to his right; a small manufactured table is to his left. Both hold the result of sheep losing their natural wool coat. Without being certain, the homemade table may also hold the man's "blade shears." The "sheep shearer" looks to be a tall young man. His dark hair is parted in the middle over a rectangular shaped face with strong cheekbones and jaw-line. The shearer looks off into the distance and not at the camera—which, in Ida's hands, is approximately fifteen to twenty degrees to the man's left. He wears well-used bib overalls over a heavy looking long-sleeved shirt. He reveals his tallness in the slight lean right at his waist, as he holds the upright, newly sheared sheep by its neck and head. The man's stance seems to convey pride in his profession. Ida has captured it well.

Luke has been shearing sheep for six years,
and familiar with Forrest Stewart's flock
for nearly that long.

Luke raises sheep of his own,
some ways up Mormon Hollow Road.
This young man doesn't get rich shearing sheep;

but he enjoys it—giving him time to think of other things
while running his shears through their wool coats.
The last sheep of Stewart's flock is just about naked.

His thoughts are on his new wife, Caroline, back at home.
*What's she doing about now? That gal loves to read.*
*Sure wish she could cook as well as she can read.*

Luke's got another farm to work
before the end of the day;
he won't be home to Caroline until evening or later.

*Oh, there's Forrest's missus . . .*
*I hear she likes to take pictures.*
*Yeah, she's got her camera with her.*

*I just know I'm gonna be her next venture.*
*Ida Stewart is a handsome woman . . .*
*but not as pretty as my Caroline.*

As Ida frames shearer and sheep in her viewfinder,
Luke looks out west toward the hills and imagines himself
riding up Mormon Hollow Road.

Caroline's got supper pretty near ready.
*Sure hope it's not fried eggs and bread again.*

## "AUNT AND LAMB, 1905"

Ida had made a note on the back of the photo's pasteboard, "Aunt and lamb." A tall, middle-aged woman stands erect on the sloping lawn of the Stewart farmhouse. Ida frames her aunt with the house behind and slanting off her left shoulder at roughly a thirty-degree angle. Aunt holds her left arm behind her back as if she senses the house moving toward her on a trajectory—afraid it would remove her limb while passing on its imagined path. Again, the gambrel-roofed horse barn is a far backdrop to the left of the picture. A lamb appears to nuzzle the hem of Aunt's dingy dress; most likely going after the tender, sweet grass of the lawn. Aunt has turned her head to the left; her serious gaze seems centered on a far off object. What did she set her eyes on all those years ago? We will never know for sure as Ida snapped the picture. Aunt does not smile, maybe choosing to appear courtly instead of friendly. Her face is pinched with sunken cheeks; perhaps she is missing her teeth. She has piled her dark hair up on her head where it forms into a top-knot. Her face possesses sharp features; we can best describe her with the old-fashioned terms: dowdy and sour. But then, we have no knowledge of the kind of life she lived.

It's second nature to Ida—
taking photos of family, friends, and neighbors.
And so, she asks her Aunt Flo to pose.

Ida's Aunt Flo, a widow—whose late husband
died of pneumonia the previous winter,
is up from Corning—

a small industrial city eight miles south of the farm.
She has come with her youngest children, a boy and a girl.
Flo has told herself, she has come to get away

from the clamor and heat of the city and
rest from a job as a laundress.
Flo, normally self-conscious, is reluctant to pose,

knowing she lacks comeliness.
She also carries grief from her husband's recent death—
feels lost, out of place in the world;

her visage reveals suffering and loss.
She has tenderly carried around a lamb
for a good part of the afternoon.
Its body next to hers, despite the early summer heat,
has been a comfort.
Flo responds, "Oh, Ida, you don't need to

take my picture." Ida shrugs and says,
"Who says I need to, I *want* to," and leads her aunt
to a spot on the farmhouse lawn

just southwest of the house.
Suddenly, Flo is unsure what to do with the lamb
and sets it down at her feet.

She is fidgety before Ida's camera.
Ida says, "Think pleasant thoughts."
Aunt Flo turns her head and gazes south toward home.

All she can see is her husband's grave
in the South Corning Cemetery.
She thinks to herself:

*I must remember to replace his flowers when we get home.*

## "WADERS IN POST CREEK, 1905"

Ada's aunt has joined a small group of children wading in the shallow waters of Post Creek. The platform bridge that crossed over the creek from the main road to the farm is in the background, a small tree at its end. Again, beyond are the barns in the far distance. In near perfect composition, her aunt is to the left of the picture, facing the camera; just behind and to the right are the children— two boys and a girl. One boy and the girl bend over with both hands submerged in the water, their sides and faces visible to the viewer. The younger boy at the far right—probably Harold—looks upon his companions' doings. Possibly, at his young age, he does not know what they are looking for—crayfish under rocks? Ada's aunt has hiked the hem of her dress above the surface of the water. What she probably does not know is a bright spot of bare shin on her right leg extends from the water's surface to the hiked hem. What did she think or say of this photo upon first seeing it!?

It's a hot enough summer day that
even Ida's Aunt Flo steps into Post Creek,
timidly wading in with the children.

Ida is already in the creek with her camera.
She is studying the scene, waiting for a good moment
to snap the ready shutter open—

recording the casual scene before her.
Ida knows her aunt's reluctance to pose for a picture,
and observes Flo idly watching the kids at play—

lifting rocks from the creek bed, looking for crawdads.
Young Harold also watches—yet, unsure of their actions.
Flo is well aware of Ida's waiting camera;

she refuses to cooperate.
"Oh, Aunt Flo, stop being bashful and stubborn.
Let me get a picture of your face."

Flo snaps, "No more pictures, Ida, stop pestering."
What Flo should know is Ida is patient, willing to wait . . .
almost five minutes pass quietly.

Flo, lost in thought and intent on keeping her
balance on the slippery rocks, forgets Ida's camera.
She has turned her face toward its waiting eye.
The photographer is ready;
looking down in her viewfinder,
she calls her aunt's name, and snaps away.

It took awhile for Aunt Flo to get over
her niece's plucky behavior.
But she finally did.

## "TRACK GANG, 1905"

Seven men stand in a row between the double tracks of the New York Central Railroad line that runs north-south some hundred yards or so behind the Stewart barnyard. Six wield flat-bottom shovels. The seventh man at the far right has his arm around a shorter man's shoulders. All wear hats with brims, as opposed to the ubiquitous ball caps or hard-hats of today. Denuded hills lay in the background. Ida has wandered out with her camera to capture on film these laborers who stand erect and proud in the midst of their work day. As noted on the back of the pasteboard, Ida calls these men a "track gang." Other names for these workers were "section hands" or "gandy dancers." Their regular job was to lay and maintain sections of track. The specific job on this day appears to be the construction of a rail crossing so farmer Stewart could get his wagons and equipment into a field beyond the tracks. Ida celebrated the event with a photograph of the men who made it possible. That same crossing existed in the mid 1980s—though not used for some time. A fallen down equipment shed lay along the farm lane beyond the tracks.

The men of the New York Central Railroad
are just about done with the Stewarts' rail crossing.
If Ida had come out with her camera any later,

they might have been gone.
Upon her approach the men stand erect
from their work, watchful.

They wonder among themselves,
*Who's this young lady coming toward them,
and what's she carrying?*

The lead man—the man without a shovel,
tells them to mind their manners, no cussing.
"I believe she's the farmer's missus."

Ida stands before them holding her camera up
like it was a message in itself,
a statement of fact without the words.

Since some look puzzled, she says, "It's a camera . . .
I'd like to take your picture."
They look among themselves as if to say—

*why would anyone want to take our picture?*
Their leader says, "Okay boys, line up for the lady,
try to look smart for once."

They grumble good-naturedly.
Then as if by some military instinct,
place their shovels before them like rifles—

one leaning on the handle with a jaunty pose;
the man on the far left stands on the rail,
projecting himself above the others.

All looks good in Ida's viewfinder . . .
but then, she says to the middle man,
"Hold your shovel up as if you're using it."

One of them calls out,
"It'll be the first time today he did!"
All laugh, and the leader suddenly

wraps his right arm around the shoulders
of the shorter worker next to him.
"Ain't this something, Ed?"

Ed replies,
"Yep, and the wife won't believe a word of it."

## POST CREEK TEMPERANCE MEETING

A group of twenty-six adults, and one baby, are gathered before a large tent. A sign, placed on the front pole, identifies them as the "Post Creek Women's Christian Temperance Union." Eighteen are women; the rest, of course, are men, the gender of the baby unknown. The top row stands while three rows sit before them in various heights. Male members are dispersed at the top and bottom—elder gents at the top, younger men sitting on the grass. Both women and men are well dressed for the occasion. As in many group photos—not all look at the camera. Ida has taken the picture about thirty degrees left of the center of the tent; it is another carefully crafted composition. It is a bright summer day with deep shadows filling both bottom corners. The right shadow—most likely made by a large tree; the left—a straight edge—possibly the outline of a roof. Tall trees fill the background. A special day perhaps? The Fourth of July? A picnic among members and interested guests? Ida has noted neither the date nor location and occasion of the meeting on the back of the photo. Possibly around 1905, it is fifteen years before women get to vote, and prohibition of alcoholic drink becomes a reality in America. At this point in the US alone, the WCTU has registered almost one hundred sixty-thousand members. Was Ida the twenty-seventh member of this chapter? Or, was she there with her camera as a curious observer? No record is known.

The Post Creek Chapter sets in for their photograph—
most truly teetotalers, others perhaps taking a nip
now and then for *medicinal* purposes.

Many appreciate the chance to get out of the hot tent,
secretly tired of the long-winded speakers
who say the same thing at every meeting—

especially the preachers among them.
Yet, this does not mean they have grown doubtful
of the mission—just weary of seeing no change.

Some are more interested in temperance than suffrage,
others just the opposite. Some share a double concern.
However, this does not matter, they are in it together.

Some are devoted Christians;
others are more like fellow travelers—
not opposed to religion if in moderation—

this being mostly a secret perspective.
Ida is more into suffrage,
but agrees strong drink can be ruinous.

Today, she has come to listen to orations
and proposed future events,
and of course, has brought her folding camera.

Ida is surprised when the president of the chapter—
the woman sitting on the grass in the front row,
far left—wearing the only dark dress—

asked her to photograph their group.
Once the simply curious see Ida's camera,
they retreat to the sidelines—possibly

away from being forever identified with the group.
After Ida has taken the photo,
the leader tells them it is time for refreshments.

At the announcement, the curious onlookers rejoin the activity.
After all, it *is* a very warm day;
they could use a glass of cold lemonade and some cake.

## GROCER F. H. COGER'S DELIVERY MAN

Mr. Coger's delivery man stands beside his van wagon—hands in pockets, wearing gartered white sleeves, neck tie, and soft cap. Two large, dark horses stand quietly before the wagon; they pull it up and down country roads six days a week. Ida has placed the driver carefully, so as not to obstruct the lettering on the wagon's side panel: F. H. COGER, and below it, GROCER. It is difficult to know the exact location of this picture, yet, probably near the Stewart farmhouse. The wagon is parked on the grass; wildflowers dot the area between subject and photographer. Partially wooded hills fill the background. Is the delivery man Frank Coger himself? Probably not, for his is a thriving business in Corning—a small city more than seven miles south. At the time of this photo he is also the treasurer of the Corning Grocers Association—elected so in 1901. Grocer vans traveled long hours out into the rural areas, stopping along the way, hoping to refresh known customers' pantries. It seems unlikely that Coger himself would be away from the store that long.

For Ben, a Coger delivery man—
it's an ordinary summer day,
traveling the country roads north of the city.

Yet, today Ida Stewart wants to take his photograph
standing next to his wagon;
it's the first time this ever happened on his trips.

Her new groceries are in the pantry,
the record of sale made in Ben's notebook,
now he's ready to mount the wagon and

head out to his next customer.
Before he can do so, Ida appears with her little camera.
"Ben, how about I take your picture with the wagon and all?"

"Why so, Mrs. Stewart?"
Ida never knows how to answer this often repeated question—
at least to her own satisfaction.

If she told folks her reason
for wanting to take photographs,
they probably wouldn't understand.

"Oh . . . just thought it would be nice.
I like taking pictures of folks here abouts."
So Ben simply says, "Okay,"

while jamming his hands into his trouser pockets.
Ida says, "Move a bit to your left, Ben.
I want you between the van and the horses."

Ben muses . . .
"That would be a dangerous place to be, Mrs. Stewart."
He chuckles to himself at this subtle attempt at humor.

Ida replies, "Oh Ben, you know what I mean."
He chuckles again, "Guess I do ma'am."

## WINTER PHOTOS: IDA, FORREST, THE HORSES, AND A SLEDGE

It's a high contrast black and white picture. Taken against a snowy winter scene, there are little, if any, gray tones in Ida's self-portrait with the farm's two horses. She stands between them, holding the bridle of a white equine in her right hand, while a dark horse appears splayfooted and free of human control. The horse barn with its cupola is seen in the far background just behind the white horse's head. At a distance behind the dark horse are winter trees, bare branches scratching at the overcast sky. Barn and trees are the only barrier between the whitened earth and the winter heavens. Ida wears a dark winter coat with hat, mittens, and boots. One can guess that Forrest, her husband, took the picture—following as best as possible her explicit instructions as to composition. In a possible companion photo we see Forrest standing in his winter sledge, pulled by his two reliable horses. The sledge is most likely filled with horse and/or cow manure to be laid out on the farm's dormant fields. He looks back at Ida behind her camera. Snow covered hills fill the scene beyond. One can only guess as to which picture came first.

Ida has retrieved their two horses from the barn,
limbering up their cold bones and muscles
for the job ahead.

She has walked them up to the house
where Forrest is searching for something
in the rear tool shed.

An idea looms in her mind:
"Forrest, why don't I take a picture
of you with your two beauties;

you sure spend a lot of time with them.
They're like family."
Forrest mumbles something within the shed;

he knows Ida wasn't asking a question.
"What you say?" she asks.
He pokes his head out the door.

"Now Ida, you know I don't like my picture taken.
And I got work to do."
Ida objects,

"Oh phew, that manure ain't gonna spoil or something
waitin' a couple more minutes."
Forrest knows his wife is formidable

when it comes to getting her way—
especially when it comes to her artistic wants.
Yet, she decides to compromise:

Forrest will take *her* picture with the horses.
Later with the sledge filled with manure for spreading,
the horses hitched up, Forrest heads for the nearest field.

What he doesn't know—
Ida has secretly followed with her camera.
She yells his name, he turns . . . the shutter opens and closes—

capturing her reticent husband for posterity's sake. The horses are totally unaware of this human comedy; it's just another work day for them.

## "THREE SISTERS, 1912"

Ida has labeled her photo "Three Sisters 1912," a tableau of three unidentified women sitting on sunlit, front porch steps. On the left is what appears to be the eldest—middle-aged, slightly plump, wearing a white shirtwaist, a brooch at the neck, and a dark skirt in which lie her forearms and folded hands. She leans slightly toward the middle and looks off to the right of the picture as if avoiding the camera's eye; her expression is one of resignation. The sister on the right is somewhat younger. She wears a dark dress and is looking at her older sister as if paying close attention to whatever she might be saying; or she's trying to get her attention. The sister in the middle is obviously the youngest. She wears a flouncy shirtwaist and light-colored skirt, while looking directly into Ida's camera. She appears to be the only one of the sisters comfortable with the occasion. Her knees are raised with her feet planted on the lower step, her hands in her lap. All three have dark hair, coiffured in the style of the times.

Mid-afternoon, a sunny summer day,
lunch is over; three adult sisters—
Ida's long time friends—Opal, Grace, and Irma,

sit on the front steps of Opal's home—
no doubt, placed there by Ida
in the viewfinder of her camera.

Opal, a widow and the oldest,
always plagued by self-consciousness, and
head-strong, refuses to look at Ida and her camera—

setting her mouth hard against her uneasy feelings.
Grace, on the far right, looks toward her older sister,
knowing Opal is struggling to be cooperative in this undertaking.

"Opal, your three-bean salad was exceptional today.
I could have had a third helping."
Irma, the youngest and unmarried, recognizes Grace's

attempt to distract Opal from her mood.
"Why yes Opal, absolutely wonderful,"
the tone of her voice, however, unconvincing.

"Oh, hush you two . . . I know what you're doing.
I don't know why Ida has to carry that . . . *thing*
everywhere she goes.

"It's no wonder she didn't take my picture at lunch—
shoveling food into my mouth like a hog!
So, now she wants to record the aftereffects

of my too healthy of an appetite."
Grace says weakly, "No Opal, you look just fine.
Besides, your cooking is hard to resist."

Opal says, "Oh, hush," and continues to look off
into the distance as Ida takes their picture.

# PART THREE

## Lost Sentiments

*Field Notes at Mid-Life*
*(1989 to 1999)*

A Celebration of the Examined Life

"Always be a poet, even in prose."
—Charles Baudelaire

"Ruminants are a perfectly normal thing to possess when you live in upstate New York. It's just moving scenery."
—Vera Farmiga, actress

"Middle-age men feel good but have a sense that there's more to life, if only they could access it."
—Max Berlinger

# Introduction
## Lost Sentiments

lost 3. Gone or passed away.
4. Uncertain; bewildered.
5. Absorbed.

sentiment. 1. a. A cast of mind regarding something.
b. an opinion or view about a specific matter.

—*The American Heritage Dictionary*

Not all agree at what age "mid-life" begins, and when it ends. Some commentators say at forty, some say before forty, others would tell you sometime after forty. My definition of mid-life began and ended with a journal I started in early 1989—just after my fortieth birthday—and ended in 1999 after leaving my secular occupation of thirty years in industrial engineering as a drafter/designer, and entering into full-time pastoral ministry. Most would say a man at fifty is still in mid-life. I wouldn't deny that; yet the particular sentiments found in the following prose pieces came from that journal of ten years—at a time of mid-life *assessment*. I truly believe I avoided the so-called "mid-life crisis" by working through my mental and emotional state by putting my thoughts on paper. These sentiments were "upstate born" while living in New York's Finger Lakes Region.

PART THREE: LOST SENTIMENTS

    One can well imagine that these pieces don't constitute ten years of journaling. A reader would become quite bored of the repeated floggings of my personal struggles at mid-life. The following verse and prose-poems represent the times when I managed to break away from dreadful self analysis and speak more generally of my experiences of the world at forty and beyond. As to the idea of these thoughts and sentiments being "lost," certainly they have not "gone away" as they are now preserved in this collection. I prefer the idea of them as being "absorbed" (see above). These sentiments (some might label them philosophies) were a part of my life; I own them. While reading and reworking these journal entries into poems, I realized—I'm still much that man in many ways, and not so in many others. Now, thirty years later, Max Berlinger's quote from above reminds me that through this work, I have achieved at least some "access" into understanding what "more to life" actually means.

## *PROLOGUE:* A MAN AT FORTY-SOMETHING

> "We are all, in some measure, Job [in the Bible], who demands an answer from mystery itself. Certainly I could never claim, as did Job, to be righteous and blameless—that in itself... is a foolish claim, that all must relinquish: we cannot be other than what we are, limited and imperfect. Yet how hard we try!"
>
> —KATHLEEN RAINE (1908 TO 2003),
> ENGLISH POET AND SCHOLAR

I.
A man at forty-something occupies a strange place in the land—happy at times to be done with the foolishness and impulses of youth; yet, at more maddening times—desiring their excitement and mourning their loss. It would be nice to believe that now I could buckle down and move forward without silly distractions, and finally accomplish great things. After all, don't we believe a "mature" man can easily separate the silly from the serious, illusions from the important? A man at forty-something must lean harder into the wind; strength is not the problem—experience tells him to get an advantage. The problem is—what might that be?

II.
The body is like a ship sailing the waters of life. Human nature—the physical and mental engine we use to journey the reality of time and space. My soul—an "I" among billions of "I's." My feelings, thoughts, desires, and my will are aboard my ship. As a man, I stand on the deck of consciousness, aware of myself in a world of other ships, other decks, other souls—some so close, but often kept at a distance enough to determine a perception of them. Here's

where my spirit and soul needs to discern the spirit of these other "I's." Often, I wonder if it's healthy enough to be up to the task.

III.

I find it's true. It's difficult to like some men upon first impression. Is it because it's the way these men present themselves? Is it what may be simply confidence, appearing as arrogance? Yet, I must admit, sometimes insecurity can be mistaken for arrogance. I have sometimes looked upon these men with a mean spirit and said to myself: *they see themselves as the sole possessors of reason, ability, and charm.* However, it seems more likely, it's the idea that these men can do something that I can't do—that bothers me. It's a strange chemistry that draws one man to another. And, it's an equally strange alchemy that causes one to make hasty or pretentious conclusions turning us from a gem to a simple stone.

IV.

I think our lives can be said to wear undergarments made of choices; under the frivolous outer garments of our external lives, we wear close to us the results of important decision making. (Are the outer garments only meant for show?) Everyday living seems to offer a variety of choices: what to believe, what to think, who to trust—with morals and ethics playing a very large part in our deciding: what is right, what is wrong? What is good, what is bad? What is true, what is false? Because serious decision making can be tough, it appears many decide to gamble and take what is forced upon them. This leaves them with the option of rationalizing the results: "What else could I do?" "How was I to know?" Nevertheless, it would seem our choices are always ours—even when we pretend they're not.

## TO TRANSCEND OR NOT TO TRANSCEND, THAT'S NOT REALLY THE QUESTION

I've been reading the lives and works of Ralph Waldo Emerson and Henry Thoreau, two of the leading transcendentalists of the early nineteenth century. To me Emerson's writings (except, perhaps, for his journal, which has moments of clarity) are at best somewhat confusing, often filled with conjecture and hyperbole. All his talk of nature, self-reliance, and emphasis on subjective intuition is often untraceable; it's hard for me to make the connections.

Yet, I find there is an attraction to these strange writings. It occurs to me that the transcendentalists longed for the freedom of the human spirit to transcend the rational, which I feel they were unable to truly obtain. For there's a constant struggle between the mundane of our everyday lives and the spiritual part of our nature. Can intuition ever *truly* free us from our limitations, our lack of understanding? Yes, we are material creatures, and yes, we are spiritual creatures. It would seem the struggle is for our spirit to live in harmony with our mind, and with the weaknesses of our body. If Emerson truly believed that human temptation was a much overrated figure in the human story, I wonder if he was truly honest with himself. Like I said, I really don't understand Emerson. It's possible he wouldn't understand me.

## UPSTATE HEAT WAVE

It's a July heat wave in Watkins Glen!
The temperature's been in the mid-nineties
for better than a week. Constant heat and

humidity over long periods of time have
an affect on the thought processes: it seems
brain cells break down and melt. Plus,

the bodies' muscles congeal, the skin's
gaskets begin to leak under the pressure—
drop by drop by drop . . . and so—people

at Clute Park at the end of Seneca Lake
have undone their civilian clothes
for the uniform of late twentieth-century

American recreation—the swimsuit—
for those who enter the lake and for those
who don't. Semi-nakedness in public is

status quo these days. I probably attract
more attention clothed. This, of course,
is a ridiculous thought; it must be the heat.

## THE CHARACTER OF TREES

I went for a walk on a familiar country road. The air was cold and damp, but the exercise of body and mind was good. A favorite tree, a maple, that had guarded the corner of a pasture, had been cut down. Three feet of trunk remained, resembling a nineteenth-century cemetery monument.

I would assume many people believe trees have no character; trees are good for shade, decoration, oxygen, and if so desired, a source of firewood. Yet, for me, a tree, though having no soul as we know it, has its own character and place in the created world. As a small boy, living in my hometown in northern Pennsylvania, our street was once lined with great American elms—majestic trees, their stature like that of aristocracy. However, one by one these tall, diseased old trees were cut down and hauled away, leaving low stumps like tables set aside the street. Our hilly neighborhood lost more than shade or ornamentation—it lost a legacy, an identification with its natural self, a connection with those neighbors who lived in, and left their houses in death. Perhaps, even more important for me, I lost a connection with *my* past. That is the character of trees.

## ONCE UPON A TIME, A SINGER, SONGWRITER

The songs I wrote in the innocence of youthful dreams have remained unsung for many years. In those heady times I had great vernal courage and desire to explore, to experience myself as a hero of popular culture. It was a time of the classic singer-songwriters—Dylan, Taylor, Young, Croce, Mitchell, Harris, Lightfoot, Rush, and others. So, I sang my songs before friends, family, and a few strangers—all the while thinking I was truly creative and profound, my words and feeble guitar strumming, touching people's souls in a mystical kind of way. Perhaps, some really enjoyed and participated in my head game in a kind of "mass illusion." Or perhaps, they were just being patient and kind in an age dedicated to *free love* and "doing your own thing in your own time."\*

Then in the summer of '73, I "performed" with my cousin Rob (who actually could play the guitar, and was a real encourager) in a makeshift "coffee house" in the basement of a Methodist church in Horseheads, New York. I got to sing into a microphone; I had hit the "big time"! Yet, looking back, I believe it was the beginning of the end of a youthful illusion. After singing a few nervous songs while forgetting many of the words, Rob and I, along with a few friends, including my future wife, drifted out the basement door. Rob and I began to play together again out on the cool concrete steps of the entrance, the summer night flooded with warm, vernal air. Down below there had been little response to my songs. Now we played our final set to the quiet, darkened street. That evening my life had suddenly begun to change. Yet, then, I didn't know it clearly enough.

\**A line spoken by Peter Fonda's character in the motorcycle movie* Easy Rider.

## A STRANGE COMPULSION

It's early March; Canada geese are heading north toward home, honking their way through overcast, late winter skies; from down on earth one can't see their flight because of low clouds and hilltop fog. The cycles of nature and time continue to roll: leaving and returning, hellos and goodbyes, living and dying—all weaving experience and memory into a sometimes quiet, sometimes chaotic pattern we call life—our days, months, and years patched together at different times and in different places—forming stories others might ever know only through conversation, memoirs, letters, diaries, and journals. We unconsciously think of *today* as being the eternal present; the moments before and the moments after take their place with us hardly noticing the succession—present time, places and people tied together with the past and a possible future by the fragile, thin line of consciousness—just like the thin lines of returning geese moving toward the future with a strange compulsion.

# MINDFUL

My eight-year-old daughter sat on the back porch
with a book in her lap, talking into the air before her.

How foolish of me not to see the rows of eager-faced
students before her as she taught them their lessons.

A child can move easily from one world to another.
Adults do this sometimes, but oftentimes, ours is not

the innocence of childhood. Many so-called "grown-ups"
often flee into fantasy in wild escape—not to expand

their horizons, but to endure for a time. The child learns
from his or her imagination, while the adult often runs

into illusion to forget lessons already experienced.

## EMELINE DAVENPORT

In early autumn I stopped at a small country graveyard off Brown Road in Schuyler County—just to browse among the old headstones. A simply carved but somehow endearing stone caught my eye. It read: "Emeline Davenport/died Oct. 7, 1831/aged 13 years." Perhaps it was the name *Emeline*, or maybe the young age of the girl—just approaching a milestone in life. It was, likely, the combination of the two. The still sharp cut of its hand-carved letters seemed to jump out of the stone at me, as if purposely trying to catch my attention. One hundred and sixty years after being carved in gray rock, Emeline's name remained bright and fascinating under a rough cut bouquet of rock-hard wildflowers. No other Davenports were buried near her; it was as if she had been abandoned, family members drifting off to unknown places.

Nothing more can be known of Emeline Davenport, a young girl who died in the early nineteenth century. How did her parents deal with her death? What of the dreams and hopes of this young miss? Emeline Davenport's dust lies immersed within the cold clay ground of Schuyler County. I feel a strange responsibility to maintain some memorial for this long-dead girl—a poem, perhaps an elegy of sorts; yet, it must be written from within my imagination, and a short life of thirteen years so long ago eludes me like the experience of death itself. It's possible I sense this strange need because I'm the father of three living daughters, and I wouldn't want *them* forgotten to the ages.

## ROADS AND JOURNEYS

My wife and I visited a friend last evening, a very talkative woman who can go on without seemingly taking a breath; she can be overwhelming. Our friend has experienced many struggles and is making the attempt to straighten out the crooked road these struggles have made of her life. Like our visit with this person, humans often come to crossroads with other people's lives. Together, at the end of our days, our journeys—the roads we have taken, would make a strange map for others to trace.

Many times our roads are thin black lines—those minor secondary roads that weave through the countryside. Traffic moves slowly; life seems simple as we take in the view as we go by. There's no hurry to get to a destination; we let the road lead us to where it wants us to go. Yet, the journey has purpose; the journey *itself* is the purpose.

Our blue-line roads can be full of life moving ahead with intention; we have a destination, we think we know where we are going. However, life is not always well organized on these blue-line roads. Often we find ourselves behind other, more slow moving lives—less motivated to get somewhere, looking perhaps for the next turnoff onto a thin black-line road. Oh, how we can get frustrated, wanting to blow our horn, and shout curses—if only within ourselves. We desperately look for an open stretch ahead, hoping to pass with a burst of speed and pent-up energy. But, lo and behold, at the next stop light or busy intersection of life—there they are right behind us! So, what's the rush?! Life on the blue-line roads can be quite unpredictable. However, that's the thrill of the journey.

Of course, there are four- or six-lane superhighways with limited access and exits. These behemoths of dark red or green lines seem to be the main arteries of the late twentieth century—moving faster and faster across endless miles of life. These roads hardly allow us to know where we are, or where we've been; the journey gets in the way of our immediate destination. Our ever increasing speed doesn't allow us to remember anything of the journey—except the tedious highway before us. What could we possibly relate to at this rate of speed?! We might be alone, but at least we feel in control—until we come to an existential crisis, those pileups at high speed, the sudden traffic jams, and the erratic driving of empty, wasted lives.

For many it's difficult to read a map and know where they are and where they are going. It's even more difficult to be a mapmaker; it requires a great deal of wisdom, and patience.

## AS ONE LOOKS AT MARRIAGE

We middle-aged men gave the wisdom of our years to a young man about to be married. Most of it was in jest; what can a man pass on in the way of knowledge that can only be gained through the toil and richness of experience? The way I see it, the young, single, and searching may see marriage as a high mountain seen from a distance. They view snow-covered peaks, gathered like wise men in the clouds and say: *There I will sit in the company of the truly mature and knowing—having tasted the secrets of married life.*

However, none of us know beforehand that the climb is long and often hard; getting up to the immense and sometimes confusing knowledge of marital being takes intention. Up there the air can be thin, reality like an avalanche of missteps and misunderstandings. Endurance, strength, caution, *and* selflessness, are required as one pulls body and soul over jutting rocks and across jagged crevices; sometimes it hurts to the point of wondering.

However, when one stops to rest—pausing to look out over the view below that passes like a colorful parade before your eyes—you relish the moments it took to get this far, and look up to the peak and know the view up there is even more breathtaking. But then, how does anyone know when they've reached the peak? One day at a time, my friend, one day at a time.

## MARKET STREET OBSERVATIONS

On an early Saturday afternoon in late November, my wife and I took a leisurely stroll down Corning's Market Street—it being a feast for the eye and mind—this touristy downtown in upstate New York. The sidewalks on both sides of the street were filled with shoppers getting a jump on Christmas buying. Others were window shoppers and gawkers like my wife and I, who just wanted to observe the scene around us.

After a while we both had the same dissenting impression: very few people were willing to give up sidewalk space; it felt like we were the only ones willing to give ground to oncoming pedestrian traffic. Were we better people, more righteous, or just wimps afraid to assert ourselves against the onslaught of aggressive humanity?! Pridefully, we decided to buck the flow; holding tight to my right arm, my wife and I experimented at "holding our own." All at once it seemed the opposing flow dissipated before us. Strange how when distressing situations are faced head-on, they lose their power—much like facing down a bully. Or perhaps more likely, this section of the street was less visited by shoppers and gawkers alike.

Later, while walking past a tavern on the east end of Market Street, I took a quick glance through the front window to see a man sitting by himself in a booth. Facing the street, he seemed completely out of touch with everything except the bottle of beer before him. It was the expression on his face that caught my attention; forlorn was his gaze that didn't appear to carry beyond the limits of himself. His eyes betrayed a lack of hope—a picture of isolation and loneliness. My glimpse was almost stolen; he may not have been the man he appeared to be—it being a quiet moment lost in thought. Perhaps, he was looking for himself, but couldn't find him. Yet, it may have been a moment or two before he went home to his family, and became the contented man he was. Whatever it was, I still felt haunted by the image I saw through the barroom window.

I was then distracted out of my momentary haunting by an older woman striding past us—wearing young, trendy gear, and raising her left arm up and down like she was trying to get someone's attention. It occurred to me at that moment—aging people look so conspicuous when trying to stay current with fashion and doing strange things with their body in public.

I know these cynical sentiments about the human condition are not what I should be thinking—especially as we come into the Christmas season. Maybe a growing distrust is seeping into my soul that may or may not have its foundation in truth. Anyway, I should show more grace in my observations of other people's lives, as I hope they would think sympathetically of my earthly imperfections.

# THE BLIZZARD

It appears the worst of the blizzard of '93 is over. Yesterday, March 13, the snow started to fall, gently at first, no wind—then falling in greater fine sheets, but still no wind. By late afternoon, a breeze picked up, and into the night velocity increased up to fifty miles per hour or more by midnight. By morning, wind-sculptured drifts peaked above four feet of snow, the world silent, cold, and colorless.

The evening before, instead of keeping Skipper, our black cocker spaniel, in her coop, I put her in the tool shed—hoping to give her more protection against the high wind and blowing snow. I would have brought her in, but she strongly dislikes staying inside the house. However, she did *not* like the confines of the shed either! Around eleven p.m.—totally afraid of the confined and unfamiliar space—she began barking and whining, the inside of the shed door evidence of her fear. I ventured outside to release her from the shed, and tie her up again at her coop—her true home, regardless of a blizzard. The high wind was a constant roar across the accumulated snow, through the trees, up against any object that got in its way. In the reflected brightness of our back porch light, the snow appeared as a solid wall of churning white moving across the barren cornfield behind our house. At that moment, I felt puny, a small part of creation struggling and groaning in its helplessness. It was as if God himself was crying out his wrath through nature's fury. But by dawn, the Almighty's voice was as still as the fallen snow.

## WEATHER REPORT

Oh for spring to come . . . cold weather,
snow, even a blizzard—a winter of seasonal
weather extending its icy tentacles into late
March—vexing to the soul and spirit as well as

the body. As a reminder of spring I pinned to
the wall over my desk a photo taken last spring
of nesting baby robins in a nearby evergreen—
small open beaks reaching skyward in anticipation

of mother's return with worm or such; a true
picture of spring. In reality, any anticipation for
spring is not yet a fully conscious thing—more
an annoyance, a clumsy feeling, a seeming lack

of coordination and inability to concentrate.
Desire for warm breezes and the fresh scent of
springtime slowly grows in the subconscious—
like a bird's instincts are triggered by the growing

light—the longer days a tantalizing prelude to
the fuller symphony of spring birdsong.
The equinox approaches with certainty, the days
and nights are slowly coming to equal lengths.

Yet, there is no certainty to the length of *my*
                    weary patience.

## CIVILIZATION

I spent a February afternoon scouring the old bones of a past civilization—hiking up in the hilly state lands between Chambers and Hornby. I felt like an explorer, perhaps an archaeologist discovering lost ruins—searching for clues to how long departed people might have lived. Here in these woods are the remains of once proud farms and homesteads—a land bought up by the state of New York during the depression of the 1930s from financially struggling owners—leaving behind remnants of houses, barns, outbuildings, and abandoned wells, many left open, making caution a smart move as one steps through nearby growth of trees and bushes.

Most of these places are all but forgotten and missed except for nearly buried stone foundations on a little rise. Little remains except for broken jars and shards of clay jugs, decaying leather straps, rusted iron implements and a surviving rose or lilac bush. Perhaps, a stray brick from a once smoke-filled chimney might show itself jutting from the heaped-up earth.

These places are quiet and empty, the lives that inhabited them—not known to the hiker or hunter who passes by on an old road or marked trail. The remoteness and loneliness of these ruins can almost bring the imagination close enough, that one may begin to listen for the stories of lives mysteriously left behind, now captured and stored in the chilled winter air. One might almost sense people's spirits that warmed themselves in framed houses, and their animals in barns and sheds—waiting for the countless times their masters would trod between house and barn—the path to and fro known like an old friend—to milk a few cows, or feed, water other livestock. If one's imagination is stirred enough by a sense of lost time, one might envision the farmer at his hedgerow surveying the few acres, atop these hills, that were his to work, and become aware of his quiet gladness and contentment—despite the weariness in his body from long hours of hard labor, and the lack of cash in his pocket. If he were a grateful man with a good heart, one could imagine him smile upon wife and kids once inside his home for the night, rejoicing in his part in creation's purpose and activity.

Admittedly, this run of imagination and thought are not familiar to everyone who would walk these woods. Thinking these thoughts does not make me a better person; yet, strangely, I feel it a privilege. However these people lived—in either happiness and goodness or bitterness and regret—a time came when the generations ceased to pass on a legacy of land, occupation, values, and memories; the land became public domain, and a way of life and certain ways may now be lost. As citizens of New York State, we now own only the remnants of a certain, almost forgotten history.

## NOTES FROM A SUMMER PARK*

I've come to this small city park to read and wait,
perhaps to write in my notebook what a summer
of sun, sights, and sounds has to offer. Kids shout

from the public swimming pool: ultraviolet rays
and heat mix with chlorine wetness to remind me
of summer days as a small boy plunging into

the cool water of *my* local pool with no muzzled
sounds of joy, nor hiding my glee, my pleasure,
as I shouted as loud as possible so my voice

would be heard among all the shouts of all the
summers to come beyond my own.

Sneakers, shorts, a stripped-off T-shirt and a cap
turned backwards jump off a ten speed bike and
race to the net: a youth has come to the local court;

he arrives in the foreshadowing of an entire life
to come. Shooting baskets is a boy's practice at
putting things in their proper place—later as a man

appearing successful and coming away with acclaim.
Yet, it's *this* moment that's most important as a
black kid in sweats, red kerchief over his head, joins

the shooter—merging into a game of one-on-one.
Then more youths come to this training ground
where they sharpen skills for a hero's world.

The vigor of youth flashes across the court like
lasers. Arms and legs pump and drive toward a
glory only they can understand. A middle-aged

man's legs are cramped from sitting and watching
while under the shade of a large maple tree. His
glory is sharing this summer day in a small city park

with fellow human beings.

*Originally published in my chapbook,* Scenes and Speculation *(Finishing Line Press), now revised.*

## DO THE GHOSTS OF OLD FARMERS STILL WATCH THE WEATHER? (A TRUE STORY)*

While walking an old country lane, now seldom used except for adventurous four-wheel-drive trucks whose owners love to decorate with splashes of muddy clay—I came upon an elderly man in bib overalls, flannel shirt, a wide-brimmed hat—his broad back turned to me in the late day sun. Milking a lone cow in the middle of a ragged and weedy field, he sat on a stool—stolid like the gray rocks that jutted from the ground around him. His brown and white companion stood equally quiet, her patience like the erosion of stone. Watching for a time, I waited for him to break his rigid pose and turn, revealing a seasoned face full of wisdom. Perhaps a glance toward me would pass on knowledge long hidden. But no, his unmoving back was all I saw.

Now I ask: Was this scene real or an apparition, a refraction of the past stranded in the slanted afternoon light now filtered via a mind gone too far afield? Was it, by some chance, a drifting, suitable moment meant to instruct the ignorant present? And if so, do the ghosts of old farmers still watch the weather through misty eyes, feel bovine teats between their spirited fingers, elemental weariness in a ghostly body? I didn't approach nor ask my spectral questions—having learned to shrug my shoulders at such audacity. The evening coming on, I walked away, the western sky beginning to glow a luminous red. Not once did I presume to tell my mysterious farmer that tomorrow's weather looked good, at least on this side of the veil.

*Originally published in my chapbook, Scenes and Speculation (Finishing Line Press), now revised.

## A SEARCH FOR THE SUBLIME AMONG THE FAR LESS THAN PROFOUND

*Nothing of great importance is too profound for anyone. It is not because it is too profound, but rather because it is too uncomfortable.*

—Paul Tillich

A professional woman, a person of high intelligence—because of marriage, a transplant from another region of the country—asked me a searching question: Did it seem like most people living in our area of the world (for the most part rural or small town) were not in tune with serious and stimulating conversation? Were their interests really as superficial as they seemed? She complained that most times she was her "own entertainment." I replied that I thought most people in this part of the world were not dense or ignorant—maybe just not interested in intellectual pursuits. Perhaps, familiarity of the ordinary *entertained* them.

I believe my answer didn't satisfy; it didn't satisfy me. This is what I didn't say then, because I hadn't time to study the question: maybe the intellectual world frightens and intimidates many people; American popular culture doesn't encourage us to think critically. Through careful manipulation we are led to follow a path in this world of perceived need—in many spheres; for some, thinking only confuses the issue.

A woman in early middle-age, she spoke of years spent in the circle of well-educated friends—talking philosophy, spirituality, the meaning of life, and other esoteric subjects. Now, in a new environment, she often felt apart from her surroundings, suffering a vague sense of isolation. Her new neighbors did not seem approachable nor did they approach. Having lost touch with this woman, I wonder if she remains a soul adrift in the hinterlands of supposed simplicity, still searching for a chance to use her mind in conversation with a few friends in a world apart from the mundane. I believe I understand her loneliness. Some people hunger for more than what is in the appetizer dish—wanting instead to share a full and stimulating meal of new ideas. Yet, perhaps, things of "great importance" is a relative term, not recognizable until the truly insignificant and meaningless have left the room, and one is left quite alone with the profound. It is anybody's guess how we will respond.

## DILL'S BALM OF LIFE

Found while wandering the state lands in the town of Hornby: one broken bottle with the embossed words—*Dill's Balm of Life*. An old town of Hornby map tells me it was nearly buried, this relic at rest in the old cellar hole of one Mr. John St. John, a New York farmer.

My first thoughts: how pretentious! Certainly quaint or antiquated. Imagine the brass to put "balm of life" on a bottle of colored alcohol! Did Mr. St. John, farmer, find this stuff the answer to all of his life's pains and aches, its sorrows, mistakes, and inconveniences?

My . . . what a bold pitch! Oh those naive folks of yesterday, those simple country folks in dire and ignorant need, relying on such foolery.
Today in an age of "evolved" intelligence and high tech—yes, urbane and learned people of science—no one is buying this kind of . . .

"snake oil." Those silly notions were long buried with our gullible ancestors. Look how far we've come . . .

There were no old television sets or personal computers in farmer St. John's cellar hole—not that I looked for these items. I found no snake oil like that which pours out of today's media mix—daily, hourly, even by the minute. No, just a small piece of a broken bottle.

Still the pitch goes on . . . all our troubles and human foibles can be soothed, pampered, hidden, or made to be non-existent. And we go for it—the snake oil that makes us beautiful, desirous, or just plain fun to be with. Oh the promises that will take away our loneliness,

our emptiness, and give us what we long for in the middle of a darker than usual night. There they are—foil wrapped and always waiting—the pills that make us happy and free, destroying the pain of living once and for all. Wonderful, wonderful; we believe it all.

Farmer John St. John kept a bottle of *Dill's Balm of Life* in his cupboard for when things got hard and tough, and his body ached with the load of work to be done. Poor Mr. St. John; we can laugh at his ignorance as we switch on our electronics to unwind and

catch up with the ever seducing, current illusions at our fingertips.

## A SUNDAY AFTERNOON AT SENECA LAKE

It's relaxation with family, time well spent—like money;
sounds as if time on our account is ledgered out as a profit
and not a debt or loss in the daily transactions of life.

Warm temperatures in upstate sunshine for late autumn—
God's present blessing on the beauty of the deepest body
of water among New York's outstretched Finger Lakes.

Few people about on the last day of October; more gulls
and mallard ducks than people—the ducks waddling up
the shoreline in small and large groups—looking for

scraps left behind—now a scarcity after the picnic season
has ended—picnic baskets put away and the concession
stand boarded up against vandals and winter storms.

A couple with a little girl, perhaps around two years,
feed ducks together. The parents pull back after a while
to watch their child toss little pieces to the begging birds.

She appears serious in her mission, crying out—
"Here ducky, ducky," to get the birds' attention. When
the bag of treats is almost empty, and the girl tired of

this game, her mother gives what is left to Sarah, our
six-year-old daughter. I'm impressed in the midst of
American life that moves at such a fast pace, that this

small observed moment is both fascinating and most precious out of all the accumulated "serious" moments in the history of the world. It occurs to me, things of beauty and joy can

happen when we look to feed our spirits and souls with the true gifts of life—realities far beyond the false ones we create for ourselves. We are strangers and pilgrims passing through

a simple, out of season, Sunday afternoon in a sunny park. We are all together, and yet still alone with ourselves— and with our God. How marvelous this given life can be!

## A CASUAL RESUME

### Original journal entry—June 14, 1992

I was born just short of the twentieth century's midpoint, arriving between two wars and coming of age during another. The years of my childhood were wrought during the Eisenhower administration, while my innocence died along with JFK in the autumn of 1963. About that time adolescence bloomed like a large red flower in the center of my body and soul—extending outward toward my head and the borderlands of my gender. Puberty was that large red blossom that for a while consumed my entire being for a time. Since then I have managed to move along the thin line of time and consciousness, occasionally bumping into circumstance and emotions like a free-falling leaf or tuff of milkweed seed drifting in the wind. My mind has soared to heights of imagination and creativity, while also plummeting into a deep hole of depression and uncertainty; my heart from bitterness and anger to the experience and grand heights of faith, hope, and love. I am somewhat the very shape of my course through life, turning and twisting like those red stripes on an old fashioned barber pole. At the moment I am a mere man surveying the trodden path I've left behind, and at the same time trying to peer into the misty shroud of an unknown future. I may need a little help along the way. May God speed as I continue on my journey—both here and beyond.

—*July 4, 2024*

www.ingramcontent.com/pod-product-compliance
Lightning Source LLC
LaVergne TN
LVHW051130080426
835510LV00018B/2328